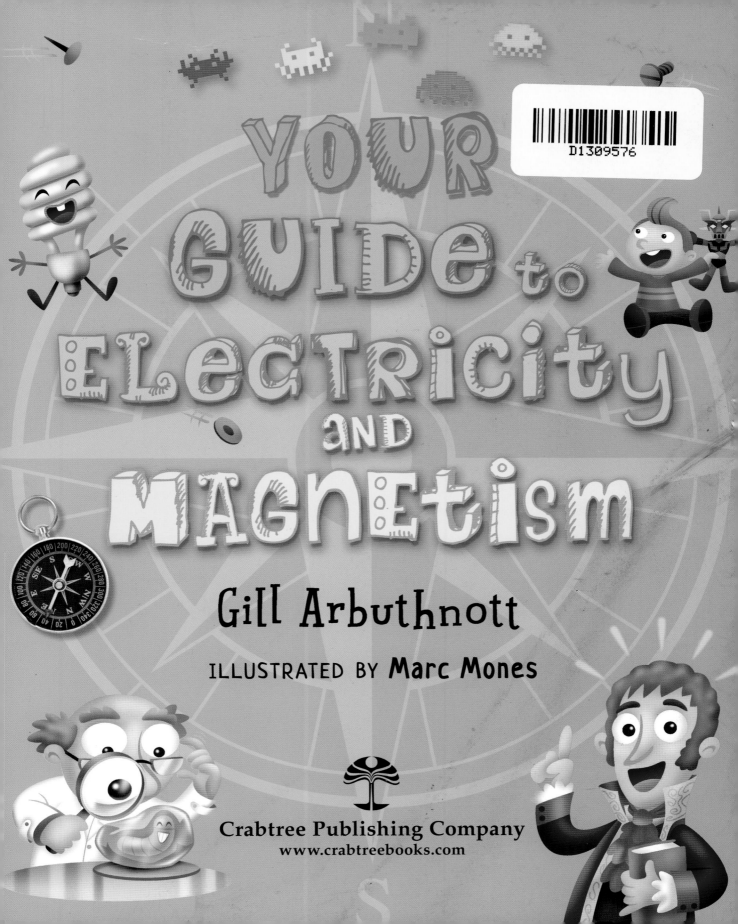

YOUR GUIDE to ELECTRICITY and MAGNETISM

Gill Arbuthnott

ILLUSTRATED BY Marc Mones

Crabtree Publishing Company
www.crabtreebooks.com

Crabtree Publishing Company
www.crabtreebooks.com
1-800-387-7650

Published in Canada
Crabtree Publishing
616 Welland Avenue
St. Catharines, ON
L2M 5V6

Published in the United States
Crabtree Publishing
PMB 59051
350 Fifth Ave, 59th Floor
New York, NY 10118

Published by Crabtree Publishing Company in 2017

To Barbara, the light of Nick's life
(even though she struggles to understand electricity and magnetism)

Author: Gill Arbuthnott

Editor: Kathy Middleton

Proofreader: Wendy Scavuzzo

Prepress technician: Tammy McGarr

Print and production coordinator: Katherine Berti

Additional images all Shutterstock, aside from the following:
Shutterstock: p17 Ambroise Tardieu, p19 Fat Jackey
Wikimedia Commons, p19 Manuel Muñoz, p22 Wellcome Trust/
Wikimedia Commons, p25 Imperial War Museum/
Wikimedia Commons, p58 "Promptuarii Iconum Insigniorum"/
Wikimedia Commons, p58 Popular Science Monthly Volume 59/
Wikimedia Commons, p58 The Life of James Clerk Maxwell/
Wikimedia Commons, p59 Wikimedia Commons.

First published in 2016 by A & C Black,
an imprint of Bloomsbury Publishing Plc

Copyright © 2016 A & C Black
Text copyright © 2016 Gill Arbuthnott
Illustration copyright © 2016 Marc Mones

Printed in Hong Kong/012017/BK20161024

Library and Archives Canada Cataloguing in Publication

Arbuthnott, Gill, author
    Your guide to electricity and magnetism / Gill Arbuthnott.

(Drawn to science, illustrated guides to key science concepts)
ISBN 978-0-7787-3398-0 (hardback).--
ISBN 978-0-7787-3399-7 (paperback)

    1. Electricity--Juvenile literature. 2. Magnetism--Juvenile
literature. I. Title. II. Series: Arbuthnott, Gill. Drawn to science

QC527.2.A72 2016   j537   C2016-906644-4

Library of Congress Cataloging-in-Publication Data

CIP Available at the Library of Congress

Contents

Introduction

Try to imagine a world without **electricity**—no phone, no video-game console, no laptop. You could get by without these things if you had to. (Yes, really!) But what if you had no light, no heat, no way to cook? We take electricity for granted. We've only known how to generate and safely use it for less than 150 years, but our modern way of life depends on it!

You might not know very much about what electricity really is, or how closely electricity and **magnetism** are linked. This book will take you on a fascinating guided tour of how we learned about electricity and magnetism, and found ways to put them to work. Want to know why a compass works? Do you know what horror story was inspired by an experiment on frogs? Want to know what the connection is between **static electricity** and dinosaurs?

Then read on!

The Mighty Atom

You can't really grasp what electricity and magnetism are until you understand **atoms**, so that's where we'll start. We begin, not with a scientist, but with a **philosopher**—someone who spends their time using reason and logic to think about ideas.

An ancient Greek philosopher named Democritus thought about what would happen if you took a piece of gold and cut it in half, then cut it in half again. If you kept on doing that, would you just get smaller and smaller pieces of gold? Or would you reach a point when it was so small that you couldn't cut it in half any more? Democritus called this tiny, uncuttable thing *atomos*. Today, we call it an atom.

Democritus was a philosopher in ancient Greece.

Gold

Democritus wasn't exactly right. Gold is called a **chemical element**, which means it is made up of atoms. But an **element** can contain only one type of atom. It can't be broken down into a simpler form. So if you cut up an atom from gold, it is no longer actually gold.

Empty space

Atoms are much too small to see, even with the most powerful microscope. Scientists had to figure out what an atom looked like by doing experiments. And guess what? It turns out most of an atom is just empty space. This is a hard thing to imagine—go ahead, just try to imagine emptiness!

Picture the whole atom as being the size of a small island. Sitting in the middle of it is a coconut. That's the nucleus, or center of the atom. Now imagine tiny mosquitoes flying around the coconut. These are **electrons** (see below). The rest of the island is empty!

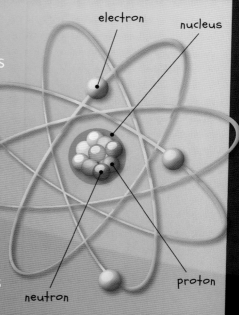

So what's in an atom?

The **nucleus**, or center, of an atom contains almost all the **mass** of the atom. It is made up of particles, or pieces, called **protons** and **neutrons**. Protons are **particles** that have a positive electrical charge. Neutrons have no charge at all. Whizzing around the nucleus are electrons—tiny particles that have a negative electrical charge. The positive charges of the protons are perfectly balanced by the negative charges of the electrons.

electron

nucleus

neutron

proton

Static Electricity

Now that you know a bit about atoms, let's look at some of the early discoveries about electricity. Back to ancient Greece first!

Amber

If you look at a pine tree, you might see sticky areas on the bark. Sometimes you can find a sticky yellowish substance leaking out of a freshly cut pine tree. This sappy material is called resin. When resin hardens, it is known as amber. The Greek word for amber is *electron* (ἠλεκτρον), which means something like "the beaming Sun." Amber can be polished to make beautiful, honey-colored stones, which are used to create jewelry. The ancient Greeks were the first to use amber that way. They also discovered that little bits of dry straw would be attracted to the stone if you rubbed it with fur. Although they didn't know it at the time, they had just discovered static electricity.

This is resin dripping down the bark of a pine tree.

> When charges move from place to place, they produce a current, or a flow, of electricity. Static means "not moving." Static electricity forms when charges build up in one place.

Try it yourself

If you know someone with some amber jewelry, offer to polish it for them. See if you can get it to pick up tiny bits of paper. (Make sure they say yes before you start the experiment!)

Don't worry if you can't get your hands on any amber. You can try the same experiment with a plastic ruler instead. Rub it hard on a wool or cotton sweater for about 20 seconds. The little bits of paper should stick to the ruler. Don't give up if it doesn't work the first time. Success can change with the weather!

Amber and science fiction

Insects sometimes become trapped in sticky plant resin. If they are completely covered by the resin, they won't rot when they die. And if the resin hardens into amber, they become **preserved** in it. This has been happening for millions of years. By looking at specimens preserved in amber, scientists have been able to study insect species that have been extinct for centuries!

The author Michael Crichton used this idea in his book *Jurassic Park*. In the story, scientists found blood-sucking insects preserved in amber from the age of the dinosaurs. The scientists were able to extract dinosaur blood cells from the insects that fed on them. The blood cells carried dinosaur **DNA**—the chemical instructions for building a dinosaur! They used it to create real, living dinosaurs for their new theme park. Could science fiction become reality? Not likely. You can't get complete dinosaur DNA from the insects.

Electric and Magnetic Charges

Hundreds of years ago, scientists had to try to explain static electricity and the idea of a charge without knowing anything at all about protons and electrons. Here are some of their early ideas, which introduced terms we still use today to describe electricity and magnetism.

Electric charges

Electric charges can attract or **repel** each other. But why does this happen? An American scientist named Benjamin Franklin came up with the idea that there are two kinds of electrical charges: positive and negative. His theory was that positive charges attract negative charges, but that positive repels positive, and negative repels negative.

What is a charge? No one really knows—not even scientists. A charge is just a **concept**, which is an idea that tries to explain how something behaves.

Magnetic charges

Magnets attract and repel, too. Because the word "charge" was being used for electricity, we use the word "poles" for magnets. Magnets have two poles called north and south. Just like electric charges, a north pole attracts a south pole, but a north repels a north, and a south repels a south.

Magnetic electrons!

When electric charges are moving, they produce magnetic fields. But this is only true when all the electrons are moving in the same direction. The electrons that whiz in circles around an atom's nucleus produce magnetic fields. However, some electrons are moving clockwise and others are moving counterclockwise. This makes them produce magnetic fields that cancel each other out. The result—the whole atom doesn't have a magnetic field we can detect.

Lightning

When frozen raindrops bump into each other inside a storm cloud, it creates static electricity (see page 8). Lightning is a very powerful discharge, or release, of this built-up static electricity. Lightning can move from one cloud to another, or it can hit an object or the ground. A strike happens when the cloud and the ground underneath have opposite charges. That creates an electric field, or space, that an arc of lightning can move through.

If lightning hits a tree, the sap inside is **vaporized** and the tree's trunk can explode. If lightning hits sand, the heat can turn the sand into a glass-like substance. There are about 100 lightning strikes every second, worldwide. The village of Kifuka in the Democratic Republic of Congo gets about 409 strikes per square mile (158 per sq km) every year.

Benjamin Franklin and the storm kite

Benjamin Franklin led a very busy life. He was an American author, politician, postmaster, diplomat, scientist, and inventor. Wow!

He had a theory that lightning was the same thing as electricity, and it could be drawn toward a metal object. A famous story says Franklin flew a kite in a storm to see if he could draw the electricity from lightning toward a metal key attached to the kite's string. However, this is an **extremely** dangerous thing to do. People have been killed doing this, so the story may not be true. Note: **NEVER** fly a kite in stormy weather.

People who tried different forms of Franklin's experiment were able to extract sparks from thunderclouds. This led Franklin to an idea. He attached a pointed metal rod to the roof of a building, and ran a wire from the rod all the way down to the ground. The metal rod attracted the lightning more effectively than the building. The electric charge ran harmlessly down the wire and into the ground. This seemingly simple idea is still used to protect buildings from lightning strikes today.

From Frogs to Frankenstein

An Italian scientist named Luigi Galvani began to experiment on frogs in the 1790s. He found that if the nerve in a dead frog's leg was touched with a piece of metal charged with electricity, the muscles would tighten and make the frog's leg twitch. He called this effect "animal electricity," which later became known as Galvanism. His theory was that animals had some sort of electric fluid flowing through their bodies. Later experiments proved that theory wrong.

Amazing electric cows!

Galvani's nephew Giovanni Aldini continued the work. He attached wires charged with electricity to the heads of dead cows. He found he could make their mouths open and close, and their tongues stick out.

Aldini also tried to bring dead bodies back to life—without any success, of course.

Frankenstein

A young novelist named Mary Godwin had read about these experiments when she was on vacation in Switzerland. She and her companions, the great poets Percy Shelley and Lord Byron, as well as writer and physician John Polidori, decided to have a competition to see who could write the best horror story. Mary remembered reading about Galvanism and the attempts to bring dead bodies back to life. This was one of the ideas she used to write what would become the famous novel *Frankenstein*. (She later married Percy Shelley and became better known as Mary Shelley.)

John Polidori used the story that Byron wrote that night as the basis for his novel *The Vampyre*—the very first novel about vampires. What a night!

The first battery

Italian scientist Alessandro Volta noticed that in Galvani's twitching frog experiments, two different metals were used to touch the nerve in the frog's leg to make the muscle twitch.

Volta tried a range of different metals and found that zinc and copper worked best to make the muscle move. Volta used this discovery to make the first battery out of discs of zinc and copper separated by paper soaked in salty water. Volta's work is the start of what we think of as electricity. Other scientists used Volta's battery to do experiments using a flow of electricity, or an electric current. Unlike static electricity (see page 8), a current could be easily controlled.

You can try a version of the twitching frog experiment yourself —but using a lemon instead of a frog! You'll find instructions on page 55. Ask an adult for permission and help before getting started.

Alessandro Volta

13

Simple Electric Circuits

A **circuit** is a path in the shape of a loop that the flow of electricity follows. Let's begin by looking at a simple circuit, such as in a flashlight. Although this is a simple circuit, the ideas we will discover are true for any electrical system.

The word "circuit" simply means something that starts and finishes in the same place, like a Formula One race circuit. Electricity can only flow if there is a complete circuit for it to travel around. If there is a break in the path, electricity will not flow. In an electrical circuit, the "road" must be made from materials that conduct, or are able to carry, electricity. In a simple circuit, this is a wire. The wire leads from the source of electricity to the item that will use it.

In the flashlight example, the source is the battery and the item using the electricity is the bulb. The switch on a flashlight acts as a roadblock. When the switch is pressed on, it closes the loop allowing the electrons to start moving.

The electrons carry electrical charge and energy to the bulb and the flashlight lights up. Pressing the switch off, breaks the path open. The electrons stop moving and the light goes out.

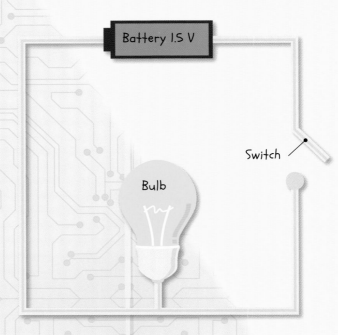

Battery 1.5 V

Switch

Bulb

But here's the puzzle: electrons move more slowly than snails! If the wire between the battery and the bulb was 4 inches (10 cm) long, it would take an electron about three minutes to get from one to the other. So why does the bulb light up so quickly? The same question applies when you flip a wall switch for a ceiling light. The switch on the wall is probably several feet away from the bulb, but when you flip the switch, light comes on instantly, too.

Pushing

So what's happening? A lot of pushing and shoving, that's what! Instead of each electron having to whizz—or should we say crawl—all the way from the battery to the bulb, the electron just gives its neighbor a push. Then that one gives the next electron a push, and so on. So it's really the push that is moving, not the electrons. When the switch is closed, the battery pushes electron number one forward. Electron one repels electron two, giving it a tiny push. Electron two does the same to electron three, and so on. Electron seven in the diagram pushes electron eight into the bulb, making it light up. Electron eleven pushes twelve into the battery—making it a full circuit.

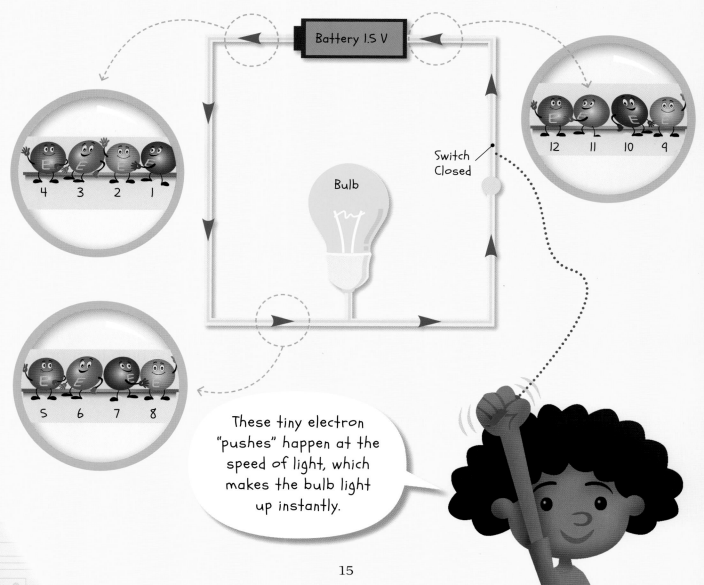

Battery 1.5 V

Bulb

Switch Closed

4 3 2 1

5 6 7 8

12 11 10 9

These tiny electron "pushes" happen at the speed of light, which makes the bulb light up instantly.

The Volt

Named after Alessandro Volta (see page 13), a **volt** is a unit of measurement in electricity. It tells us how much energy an electric charge has. This is called its voltage. You may hear someone say, "The number of volts running through the circuit is…." But this isn't accurate. It's like saying, "The height running through the mountain is…." Heights don't run, and neither do volts. There is no Usain Volt!

Volta

What is a volt?

So what is a volt? Imagine you are in a building with stairs and an elevator. You carry a tennis ball up one floor in the elevator, and let it bounce back down the stairs to ground level. A battery is like the elevator in this example. It brings energy to another thing— in this example, it's the ball. In electrical terms, it would be an electron.

As the ball bounces down the stairs, it loses energy. It's the same thing in a circuit. As a bulb uses electricity, the electrons use up their energy. The voltage is the pressure that forces electrons through a wire. In this example, the voltage is the height you take the ball up in the elevator. More height means higher voltage. The distance the ball will come down the stairs is the same as the distance it went up in the elevator.

What is an amp?

No, not an amplifier for your electric guitar! **Amp** is short for ampere. It is the unit we use to measure electric current, or how much charge is flowing around a circuit.

You might have heard of Hans Christian Anderson, who wrote fairy tales.

He had a friend called Hans Christian Oersted (that must have been confusing) who was a scientist. Hans the scientist saw that an electric current would make a compass needle move. He realized it must be creating a magnetic field.

No, I'm Hans Christian!

No, I'm Hans Christian!

André Marie Ampère

French scientist André-Marie Ampère was very interested in this discovery. He wanted to know more about how magnetic fields and electricity are related. He spent a long time doing some very complex math to figure out how strong the magnetic field is around a wire that has an electric current flowing through it. This measurement is named after him.

Magnetic Elements

All atoms produce magnetic fields, but not many elements are magnetic. Elements are pure substances that contain a single type of atom.

In elements that are magnetic, the atoms clump together and the electrons move around them in a wave, sort of like fans in a stadium. This creates a magnetic field around the group of atoms. Iron is the most well known magnetic element. It can be made non-magnetic if heated up to a certain temperature. At that temperature the magnetic fields produced by the atoms point in random directions and cancel each other out.

In iron that is magnetic, the magnetic fields produced by the atoms all point in the same direction. (Turn to page 54 for instructions on how to make your own magnet.)

Elements with the same type of magnetic fields as iron are called ferromagnetic materials. This word comes from the Latin word for iron, which is *ferrum*. There aren't many magnetic elements. Nickel and cobalt are ferromagnetic, and so are some more exotic metals such as gadolinium and neodymium.

TRY IT YOURSELF

Coins used to be made out of pure substances. For example, the nickel used to be made out of, well, nickel. Today, most coins are made from a combination of materials, called **alloys**. An alloy is a mixture of two elements, in which at least one of the elements is a metal.

Ever compared a US quarter with a Canadian quarter? They have the same shape and weigh about the same. But try placing a magnet next to both of them. Only the Canadian quarter will stick. Why? Because, since 2000, Canadian quarters have been made mostly out of a steel alloy. Steel contains iron and is magnetic. Since 1965, US quarters have been made mostly of copper, a non-magnetic material.

US quarter

Canadian quarter

How do modern vending machines detect fake coins? Light sensors measure the coin's size and electromagnets detect the type of metal the coin contains.

Earth's Magnetic Field

Earth's **core** contains a lot of iron. The very center of Earth is a solid ball of metals, and a thick layer of **molten** iron and nickel surrounds it.

These two layers are very, very hot—probably about as hot as the surface of the Sun, which is almost 10,000 °F (5,500 °C). But the middle stays solid because of the enormous pressure it's under. The liquid part of the core flows around the solid part in one direction. Remind you of something? This is like a giant version of electrons rotating around the nucleus of an atom. The flow around Earth's core produces a giant magnetic field in the same way.

Magnetic field

Crust

Mantle

Outer core

Inner core

I always wondered what was really at the center of Earth.

Did you know there are two North Poles?

Amaze your friends with this strange fact: the magnetic North Pole and the geographic North Pole aren't in the same place! They aren't always the same distance apart either because the magnetic North Pole wobbles around by as much as 10 miles (16 km) a year as Earth's magnetic field changes. It does this because the molten, swirling part of the core has currents, just like the oceans, and these change from time to time.

A fact you'll flip over!

Geophysicists looking at hardened samples of ancient lava discovered that Earth's magnetic field flips every so often. The geographic locations of the North and South poles stay the same, but the magnetic North Pole becomes the magnetic South Pole, and vice versa. This happens about once every 500,000 years—and it looks as though the next flip is due soon. Well, soonish—within the next few thousand years, anyway! Would this matter? It would certainly be confusing for animals that navigate using the magnetic field, but would it affect us?

Earth's magnetic field is getting slowly weaker, something that scientists believe happens in the years leading up to a flip.

Since the magnetic field usually protects Earth from dangerous **radiation** coming from space, we could be affected. Power and communication systems could be damaged. Don't worry though. We probably still have a few hundred years to prepare for a reversal of the magnetic poles.

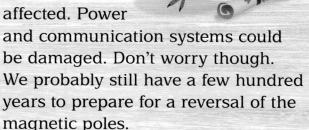

Compasses

The first compasses were invented in China about 2,000 years ago, but they weren't used for finding direction. They were used for fortune telling and feng shui, which is a way of deciding the best and luckiest places to build houses, and to design and decorate rooms and other spaces.

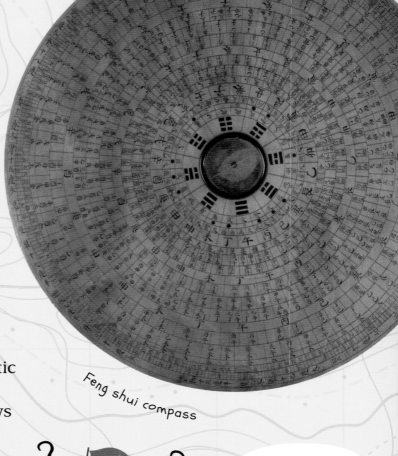

Feng shui compass

The first compasses were made from **lodestone**, a naturally magnetic iron **ore**. A piece of lodestone hanging from a thread would always turn to point in the same direction. In reality, the stone is lining itself up with Earth's magnetic field. In later compasses, magnetized iron needles replaced the lodestone.

I think we're lost, Captain!

Before compasses were available, it was very dangerous to sail out of sight of land. You could change direction without realizing it, and you might never find your way home again!

Compass confusion!

Does this all make sense? Well, hang onto your hats! We determined that Earth has a magnetic field, basically making it a huge magnet. That means it must have a North Pole and a South Pole. It's obvious where they will be, right? The North Pole is in the North, and the South Pole is in the South. Absolutely right—*geographically*. But the magnetic North Pole is at the geographic South Pole, and the magnetic South Pole is at the geographic North Pole.

> Don't panic! Here's the explanation.

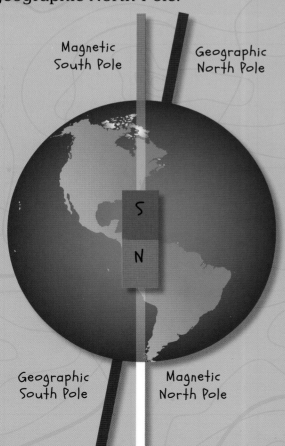

Magnetic South Pole

Geographic North Pole

S

N

Geographic South Pole

Magnetic North Pole

The geographic North Pole is the direction in which the North end of a bar magnet points if you suspend it from a string. So, if the North Pole of a magnet is attracted to it, it must be a South Pole. Remember what we discovered on page 7: North and South attract each other, North repels North, and South repels South.

A compass needle is a tiny bar magnet arranged so it can spin inside the compass and point along Earth's magnetic field. The North Pole of the compass needle is attracted to the South Pole of Earth's magnetic field. Need to lie down now so your brain can recover?

What's that Light in the Sky?

We are very lucky that Earth has a magnetic field. The Sun is a giant ball, made up mostly of hydrogen. Eruptions on its surface, similar to exploding bombs, regularly hurl huge quantities of **radioactive** particles, or pieces of radiation, at Earth. The magnetic field acts like a shield and deflects these particles away from Earth's surface toward the poles.

Aurora borealis

The Northern Lights

You can see this deflection of radiation if you are lucky enough to see the Northern Lights, if you are north of the equator. If you are south of the equator in Australia or New Zealand, it's the Southern Lights.

Also called the aurora borealis, the Northern Lights are caused by the interaction between these radioactive particles and the oxygen in Earth's atmosphere. The particles get pulled around by the magnetic field. It appears as beautiful, wavy curtains of green, purple, or red light.

The best places to see the Northern Lights are in Iceland, Greenland, Alaska, and the northern parts of Canada, Russia, and Scandinavian countries.

Animal magnetism

Homing pigeons are birds that are trained to find their way back home after being released many miles away. But how do they find their way? They can't read maps or use satellite navigation. They might be flying from somewhere they've never been, so they can't use familiar landmarks to guide them along their way.

The reason they can find their way is because they are using Earth's magnetic field to navigate. We now know that pigeons and many other birds have magnetic particles in their skulls, which help them detect the magnetic field—something humans can't do.

Homing pigeons from WWII

Homing pigeons

Homing pigeons have been used for hundreds of years to deliver messages and send news. They were an important method of communication during World War II, and some of them were even awarded medals for bravery.

Scientists are now finding more and more types of animals with this extra sense, called **magnetoreception**. It has been found in bacteria, fruit flies, salamanders, and turtles. No one understands exactly how it works yet.

What Do Magnets Do for Us?

Loads of things! For starters, have a look at your fridge door. It has a rubber seal around it. Inside the seal is a magnet, which is attracted to the fridge because the metal in it contains a lot of iron. This allows the door to be tightly sealed when you shut it. This prevents the food in the fridge from being warmed up by the heat in the kitchen

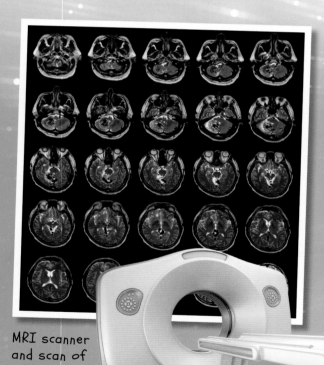

MRI scanner and scan of a brain

MRI scanners

In hospitals, doctors might request an MRI scan of a patient. MRI stands for Magnetic Resonance Imaging. The patient lies down in a machine shaped like a tube, which has a big coil of wire around it. Sound familiar? This coil produces a huge magnetic field, which alters the way electrons spin in atoms. During a scan, radio signals can detect this change and use it to build a picture of the organs inside the patient. The doctor is able to see if something is wrong without having to do an operation.

It doesn't hurt at all, although the machine is incredibly noisy. It's like lying down while someone is using a jackhammer next to your head! You do have to lie very still for quite a while. You aren't allowed to wear jewelry in the scanner because anything made of gold will get very hot, and the magnet will also pull off anything containing iron. You can't have an MRI scan for the same reason if you have a metal hip or a **pacemaker** for your heart.

The biggest experiment in the world

A scientific research organization called CERN has a ring-shaped tunnel that is 328 feet (100 m) underground and more than 17 miles (27 km) long. It would take an Olympic athlete about 90 minutes to run around it!

The letters CERN stand for French words. In English, they mean European Organization for Nuclear Research.

CERN laboratory in Geneva, Switzerland

This tunnel, called the Large Hadron Collider, or LHC, has 6,000 magnets, each stronger than the magnet in an MRI scanner. Called a particle accelerator, it is used by scientists to steer particles (protons) around the tunnel at high speeds. In 2012, experiments with the LHC were successful in observing a particle called the **Higgs boson**. Although scientists thought it existed, no one had ever seen it before. It took the LHC, which has the two biggest magnets in the world, to see it!

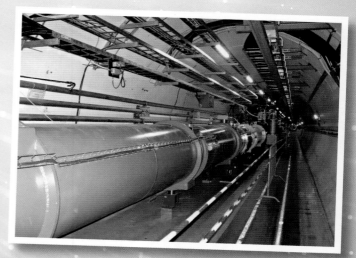

Large Hadron Collider tunnel at CERN

Electricity from Magnets

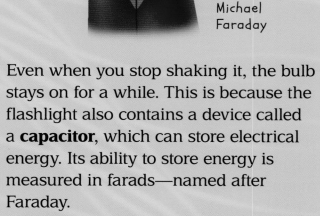

Ampère

Oersted

Michael Faraday

Scientists are always building on each other's work. Michael Faraday knew that Oersted and Ampère (page 17) had shown that an electric current could produce a magnetic field. *Aha!* thought Faraday. But does it work the other way around? Will a magnetic field produce an electric current?

Faraday's discovery

Faraday discovered that a coil of wire wrapped around a magnet will produce a current, but only if one is moving and the other one isn't. You can watch this happen in flashlights that have a magnet and a coil of wire in the handle. To make them work, you just shake them. The magnet moves inside the coil of wire and the bulb lights up.

Even when you stop shaking it, the bulb stays on for a while. This is because the flashlight also contains a device called a **capacitor**, which can store electrical energy. Its ability to store energy is measured in farads—named after Faraday.

Once Faraday had made his discovery, people quickly designed devices called **generators**. These are machines that use **rotation** as the form of movement to produce an electric current. They either rotate a magnet inside a coil of wire, or a coil of wire inside a magnet. It makes no difference which way you do it!

Good grief! I've invented the motor!

Then Faraday had another, *Aha!* moment. If movement between a magnet and a coil of wire produces electricity, could electricity produce movement? The answer was yes! Faraday had just invented the electric motor. His motor didn't work very well, but he had to leave something for the other scientists to discover.

Today, we use electric motors everywhere. If you set a cell phone on vibrate, it's using an electric motor. So is the fan that stops a laptop from overheating, and the motor that makes the hard disk on a computer rotate. And, of course, electric cars have electric motors instead of gasoline-powered motors. Then there are video game consoles, washing machines, hairdryers, food processors... The list goes on and on.

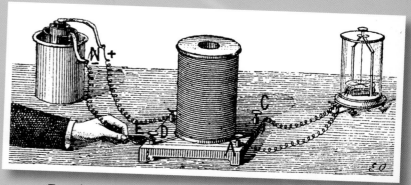

Faraday's electromagnetic motor

I wonder how many electric motors are in your house?

29

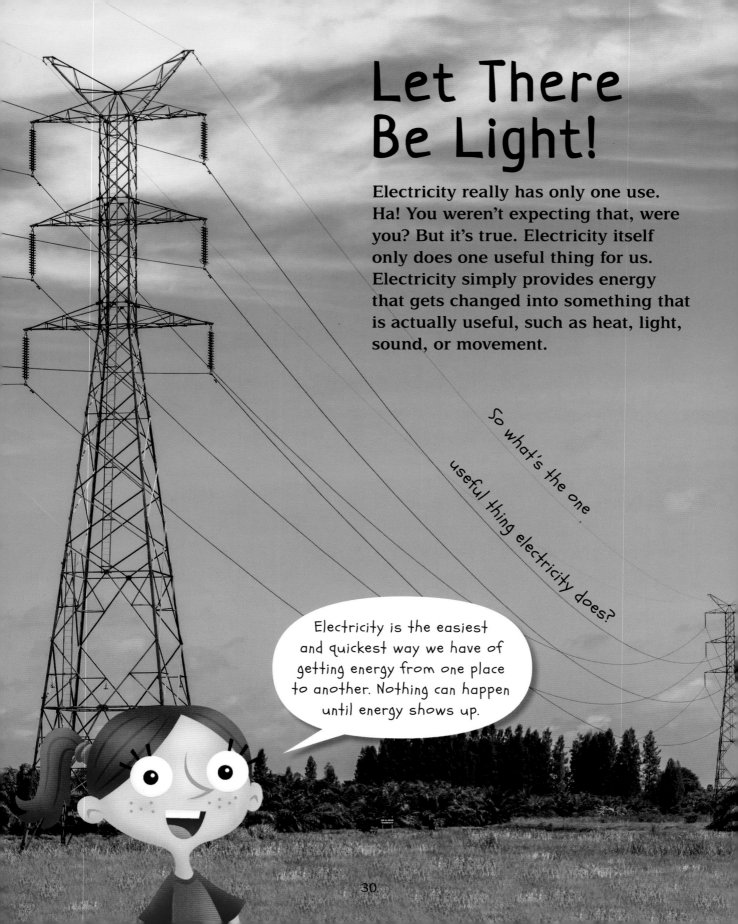

Let There Be Light!

Electricity really has only one use. Ha! You weren't expecting that, were you? But it's true. Electricity itself only does one useful thing for us. Electricity simply provides energy that gets changed into something that is actually useful, such as heat, light, sound, or movement.

So what's the one useful thing electricity does?

Electricity is the easiest and quickest way we have of getting energy from one place to another. Nothing can happen until energy shows up.

Who invented the lightbulb?

Most people who think they know the answer to this question will say American inventor Thomas Edison. You can tell them they're wrong! It was actually a British chemist named Joseph Swan. Swan's bulbs weren't very good, but they were good enough to light his house, as well as the Savoy Theatre in London, which was the first public building in Britain to have electric light. When Swan gave his friend, Lord Armstrong, bulbs to light his huge house, Armstrong wasn't impressed. The light was too dim.

Joseph Swan.

He realized this was because the generator he had wasn't producing enough electrical energy. So what did Armstrong do? He redesigned it!

Thomas Edison

What did Edison do?

What Edison did was modify Swan's design and make a better bulb. Many people still use this type of bulb today. It has a very thin wire inside, and when an electric current is passed through it, it gets very hot. It reaches more than 3,600 °F (2,000 °C). The wire becomes white-hot and produces light.

Edison's lightbulb from 1882

Which Lightbulb?

There are several different types of lightbulbs available today. Which bulbs do you use in your house?

Incandescent bulbs

These were developed by Swan and Edison (see pages 31 and 34). Inside the glass bulb is a coil of thin wire, made of the metal **tungsten**, and an **inert** gas. Inert means the gas doesn't cause a change when it comes into contact with the wire. When a current passes through the wire, it gets so hot that it glows and gives off light. However, it's very inefficient, which is why we are being encouraged not to use them any more. Only about 5% of the energy these bulbs use is turned into light. The rest is changed into heat. Halogen bulbs work in a very similar way.

Low-energy bulbs and fluorescent tubes

Low-energy bulbs and **fluorescent** tubes are the same types of bulbs, only made in different shapes. Electrons belonging to atoms of mercury inside the bulb are given enough energy to give out ultraviolet, or UV, light. Invisible to us, UV light hits a special coating on the inside of the bulb and is converted into visible light. These bulbs use less than one third of the energy of an incandescent bulb, and last for years. However, they can take up to a minute to reach full brightness, and the mercury they contain is **toxic**.

LED bulbs

These tiny bulbs are increasingly being used in flashlights, and are now starting to be used as replacements for low-energy bulbs in household lights. The letters LED stand for light-**emitting** diode. An LED gives off light when electrons move around within it. These bulbs use even less energy than low-energy bulbs, and can last for up to 20 years! The scientists who invented these bulbs were awarded a Nobel Prize in 2014.

DC and AC: The War of the Currents

No, not the sort you make jam out of—those are cur*r*ants! These are electric currents, and there are two types, called DC and AC.

Once electric lighting was invented, a way to supply the electricity was needed. Thomas Edison designed and built generators to do this. Although these generators were inefficient, they were good enough to be used to provide New York City its first electric lights.

Direct Current

Edison's generator used a Direct Current, also known as DC. This is the type of current you get from batteries. A battery pushes the current around the circuit. The voltage in the circuit is not very high, which makes it reasonably safe.

But it's not very efficient because the wires heat up. If you try to send electricity far away, most of the energy gets used up creating heat. Hardly any energy is left to make light. So a bulb's light would be dimmer the farther from the source it was.

Alternating Current

Another scientist named Nikola Tesla was also living in New York at that time. He thought that Alternating Current, or AC, would be much more efficient. This is where the generator pushes and pulls the electrons. (You can find out why it's more efficient on pages 38–39.) Tesla started to build generators that produced AC currents.

Angry Edison

Edison was furious when he heard about Tesla's AC currents. If AC became more popular to use than DC, Edison wouldn't make money from his DC generators! He tried to persuade politicians in New York that AC was too dangerous to use. He even killed stray animals with AC to demonstrate this! He did a lot of other dangerous things to try to persuade people to use his DC current. One idea even led to the invention of the **electric chair**.

Tesla comes out on top

Despite Edison's complaints, Tesla's system was much more efficient, and the AC system was widely used. The high voltage created by AC can be extremely dangerous, and you must **never** experiment with it. Tesla's name lives on today. We use his name as a unit for measuring magnetic fields.

Thomas Edison

Nikola Tesla

Generating Electricity in Power Stations

Generators work by rotating a magnet inside a coil of wire, or a coil of wire inside a magnet. But what makes these parts rotate? In most power stations, a fan is connected to the part that needs to be rotated. Steam is created and blasted at the fan to make the fan spin, which in turn makes the magnet or the wire rotate.

To make steam you need heat. Where do you get that?

Wind turbines don't need steam, but they do need wind. No wind—no electricity.

Making steam

But to make steam, you need water and heat. Power stations can create the heat they need by burning coal, oil, or gas. The disadvantage with burning these is they produce **greenhouse gases**. Power stations can create heat by using uranium to generate **nuclear power**, but this leaves behind dangerous toxic waste. Wind generators don't need steam, so they can produce heat without leaving waste that harms the environment.

Just water works, too!

You can generate electricity with just water and no heat. But the water needs to be stored high up so it can build up energy from running downhill, or dropping from a great height. This energy is used to make things rotate. This is a clean way to generate electricity, but you have to live somewhere hilly with a lot of water, such as Niagara Falls. If you live somewhere flat and dry, such as the desert, you're out of luck. The motion of ocean waves and tides are also being used to generate electricity.

Electricity generated by falling water is called hydroelectricity.

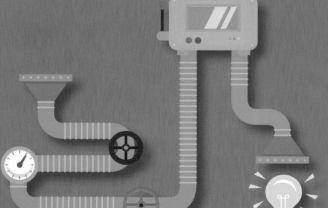

Energy in, energy out

We can't get electrical energy from nothing. First, we need another form of energy, called mechanical energy, that we can turn into electrical energy. Mechanical energy is energy created by movement. The more electrical energy we want to create, the more mechanical energy we have to put in.

Distributing Electricity

Power stations generate electricity at high voltages, which would be too dangerous for use in a household. This is why electricity is carried by two wires positioned high above or under the ground. When it gets to where it will be used, such as a house, the electricity is converted to a low voltage by a device called a **transformer** to make it safer.

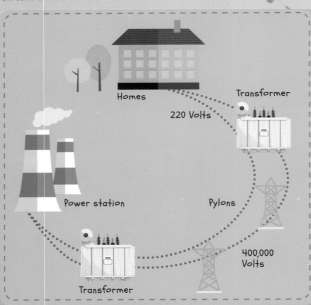

Homes

Transformer

220 Volts

Power station

Pylons

400,000 Volts

Transformer

This may look complicated, but it is really just a huge version of a simple circuit like the one in a flashlight (see page 14).

There will be a transformer somewhere near your house. Don't **ever** go near it. It's a dangerous device.

What's going on in that wall?

Modern outlets in a house have three holes in them. This is what they are for:

· Behind the hole on the right is the wire going back to the power station. You need this to make a complete circuit or the electricity won't flow.

· Behind the hole on the left is the wire coming from the power station.

· The hole at the bottom is a safety device and normally doesn't conduct electricity.

Death-defying feathered friends...

If electricity is so dangerous, then how can birds sit on the wires that carry it without getting electrocuted? As long as they touch only one wire, they don't complete the circuit, so the electricity doesn't flow through them. If they touched both wires, however, they would be killed.

When a lot of eagles were dying in the United States, they realized it was because some eagles' wingspans were so big, they could touch both wires at once. The solution was to increase the distance between the wires on pylons to make them farther apart.

Some power companies have been fined millions of dollars because protected birds were being killed by their power lines.

Electric Animals

Animals can certainly be killed by electricity, but Galvani thought there was a special kind of electricity in living things that was different from regular electricity (see page 12). He was wrong about it being different, but he was right about electricity existing in animals. Many animals have a nervous system that carries electrical signals. The energy in the signals is extremely tiny. They are measured in millivolts (thousandths of a volt). Compare this to the electricity supply in your house, which is 220 volts.

Electric eels

Electric eels live in South America, in muddy fresh water. They use electricity for hunting, defense, and communicating with other eels. Electric eels produce electricity from special organs that fill 80% of their body. It's like a living battery, which can produce up to 650 volts. But the electricity is only produced for a fraction of a second, which means it would be unlikely to kill you, even if you touched one.

It's probably best not to test this, though!

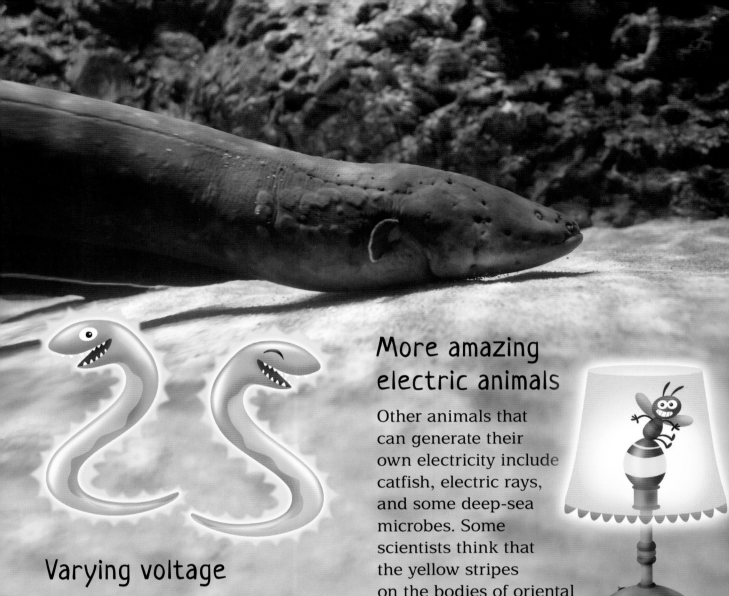

Varying voltage

The eels can alter the voltage they produce, depending on what it's for. They use a small charge (under ten volts) to navigate and locate their prey, and a much higher voltage to hunt. It's not entirely clear why they don't give themselves shocks. One theory is that because the electric pulse lasts for such a short time and the eels are such large animals, it doesn't have much effect on them. But it will stun smaller fish nearby.

More amazing electric animals

Other animals that can generate their own electricity include catfish, electric rays, and some deep-sea microbes. Some scientists think that the yellow stripes on the bodies of oriental hornets act like tiny **solar** cells that generate electricity!

Electric ray

41

Fossil Fuels

Most of our electricity is generated by burning **fossil fuels**. But what exactly are fossil fuels? Fossil fuels are coal, gas, and oil. They formed underground from the fossilized remains of animals and plants that died millions of years ago.

Oil and gas

Oil and gas are formed from the remains of tiny, one-celled plants and animals that lived in lakes and seas millions of years ago. When they died, they fell to the bottom of the lake or seabed, were buried under layers of mud, and became altered by **exposure** to high temperature and pressure.

Coal, gas, and oil

A fossil

This process is called fossilization.

42

Coal

Coal formed from plants that grew in swampy areas during the Carboniferous Period, about 300 million years ago. When the plants died, they transformed into a material called peat, instead of just decaying. Over a very long period, high temperatures and pressure turned the peat into coal.

Sometimes you can still see traces of fossil leaves on a lump of coal.

Problems with fossil fuels

There are three main problems with burning fossil fuels to make electricity:

1. We are using them up much faster than they can form. This means they will eventually run out.

2. Burning fossil fuels releases a huge amount of carbon dioxide, which is a greenhouse gas that contributes to climate change.

3. Burning fossil fuels releases soot particles and sulfur dioxide gas. Both can damage your lungs and buildings. Sulfur dioxide also contributes to acid rain, which damages plants and aquatic animals.

The effects of pollution from burning fossil fuels can be seen on city buildings.

Renewables

We need to find other ways to generate electricity, not only because Earth is running out of fossil fuels, but because they are so damaging to the environment. What we really need are clean sources of energy that won't run out.

Called renewable resources, these include energy such as sunlight and wind. The problem we must solve is how to store the energy until it's needed. For example, you can use solar power to generate electricity during daylight, but you have to store it if you want it to power your lights at night.

Wind power

On hillsides and offshore, you can now see huge wind **turbines**. They look like big fans. The windier it is, the more power they generate, which is why they are built in these places. One problem: it isn't always windy. We could never rely on wind power alone for our electricity.

Sunlight

Solar panels can convert light into DC current. Some buildings have solar panels on their roofs to supply part of the energy the building uses. You can buy solar-powered calculators, toys, and electronic gadgets. There are even solar-powered flashlights!

Some people also think the turbines are ugly and pose a danger to birds.

Hydroelectric power

Hydroelectric power means using the energy of moving water. Dams can be built across rivers to make the water flow in a controlled way through turbines, which generate electricity as they turn. People have used moving water as a source of energy for centuries. Water powered the first mills to turn huge stones that ground grain into flour. The first hydroelectric power plant designed by Tesla began to produce electricity in 1881 near Niagara Falls in the United States. The electricity was used to power streetlights in New York City. Hydroelectric power now supplies almost 20% of the world's electricity.

Remember, the greater the height the water falls from, the more energy we get.

Wave power

Waves contain enormous amounts of energy. Engineers are finding ways to harness it. This technology is still new, however, and isn't yet being used to generate electricity for general use. One of the problems is that waves are very unpredictable. Ocean tides are much more reliable. Tides go in and out twice a day, regardless of the weather. Engineers are working on harnessing energy from the movement of tides, too.

Strong waves crash over the shore.

Other Renewable Fuels

Here are some other ways that we can generate electricity. They all have advantages and disadvantages.

Geothermal energy

Earth contains a lot of heat energy, but it's difficult to get at it. However, people have been using Earth's heat energy for centuries, bathing in hot springs and using the hot water to supply public baths and underfloor heating. This is called geothermal energy. It is now being used to generate electricity in a number of countries that have hot springs. Iceland generates 30% of its electricity this way. In Iceland, the heated water is above or close to the surface of the ground, which makes it easier to use.

Is that my poo?

Biomass

Biomass is simply a word for any animal or plant remains that can be burned to generate heat energy. This energy can be converted to electricity. The most common biomass material used is wood. Other examples are straw and chicken manure.

Hot springs can also indicate that an area might be subject to volcanic eruptions!

Biofuels

Biomass can also be converted into fuels such as ethanol and methane. These are called biofuels. Methane is released by rotting animal and plant material—and also by belching cows—and is sometimes called biogas. Imagine it! Could cows be trained to belch methane into your car's fuel tank in the future?

One biofuel, called biodiesel, can be made from vegetable oil that has already been used for frying food. Researchers are also looking at algae (basically pond weed) to produce a number of biofuels.

Problems with biomass and biofuels

Both of these sound like great ideas, but they have disadvantages. Some edible crops such as corn and sugar cane are now being grown specifically to produce bioethanol. It takes a lot of resources, such as water and land, to grow these extra plants.

Some palm trees are grown for their oil. At one time, the oil was only used in foods. Now it's also being used as a source of biodiesel. Huge areas of natural forest in countries such as Indonesia and Malaysia have been cut down so that oil palm trees can be grown instead. The destruction of animal habitats has threatened endangered species such as the orangutan and the Sumatran tiger.

Deforestation in Malaysia threatens the natural habitats of many endangered species.

Transistors

The introduction in this book mentioned some of the modern devices that use electricity that we all take for granted.

Televisions, computers, video game consoles, cell phones—the list goes on and on. These have all been made possible by an accidental discovery in 1947 of an electronic component called the **transistor**.

A transistor is an electronic switch. Before transistors, switches were mechanical and had to be pressed:

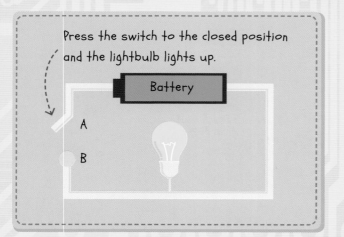

Press the switch to the closed position and the lightbulb lights up.

Battery

A

B

A transistor does the same job, but you don't need to press it:

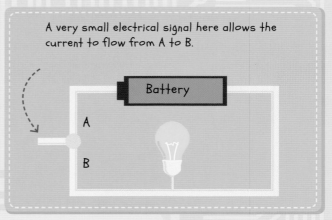

A very small electrical signal here allows the current to flow from A to B.

Battery

A

B

The first transistors looked a bit like a baked bean with three legs (but no tomato sauce). You can still buy transistors like this, but it's now more common to find them built into integrated circuits (see page 50). Today's smartphones have more than a billion transistors in them. Computers have as many transistors in one box as there are people on Earth!

Why do we need so many electronic switches?

Look at a computer screen. The picture is made up of a lot of tiny dots called **pixels**. Each dot can be switched on or off, and this is done by at least one transistor for each pixel, and usually more, since the color of each pixel can be changed from red to green to blue. So, to make a clear moving picture, you need a lot of dots switching on and off and changing color very quickly. Obviously, this takes a huge number of transistors.

Think about that the next time you watch a funny cat video on the Internet!

Semiconductors

The first transistors were made from an element called germanium. After a few years, silicon became more popular for making them, partly because it's so common. In fact, it's the most common element on the surface of Earth. Germanium and silicon are called semi-conductors. Semi-conductors are materials that get better at conducting electricity as they become hotter. Ordinary conductors, such as metals, actually get worse at conducting electricity as they become hotter.

Silicon chip.

Integrated circuits

By the 1970s, scientists were making integrated circuits. These are big circuits made by adding together lots of little circuits. Integrated circuits have millions of transistors in them on a piece of silicon the size of your little fingernail! This made it possible to make computers small enough to fit in your hand.

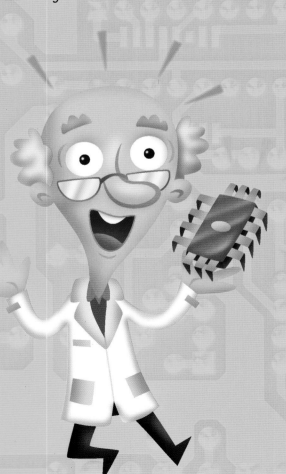

50

Silicon Valley

A lot of the early work on integrated circuits and computers was carried out in a region of California which became known as Silicon Valley. Technology-based companies such as Google, Apple, eBay, and Intel are based there or were started there.

Those pesky chargers...

A disadvantage of semi-conductor integrated circuits and all the products made with them is that they need a DC power supply. Sometimes this is just a battery, but you often need an electronic box to convert the AC supply in your home to DC to recharge your devices. This is why a charger for devices such as cell phones are often bigger than ordinary plugs.

The Future

It's been 200 years since Galvani and Volta discovered electricity, and we are still finding new ways to harness and use electricity. Here are some exciting inventions currently being developed. Which ones do you think you'll be able to buy and use in your lifetime?

Superconductors

These are usually very cold materials, which conduct electricity without getting hot. We have known about them since 1911, and they are now used in devices, such as MRI scanners. At CERN, a lot of research is being carried out to find materials which will superconduct at room temperature.

Artificial intelligence (AI)

Researchers are trying to develop computers that generate their own programs and make their own decisions. Before it was a reality, AI had long been a part of science-fiction literature. Now, it is becoming science fact.

Robots

Robots are a mix of some of the earliest electronic devices such as motors, and modern devices such as computers. Becoming more sophisticated all the time, it's possible that within a few years, robots that help with childcare and looking after elderly people will be common. The most advanced robot in existence at the moment is called ASIMO. It can walk, run, dance, climb stairs, and even serve drinks!

Wearable technology

"Tech togs" are pieces of clothing or accessories that incorporate computers and electronics. There are already smartwatches, but how would you like a pair of pants with a keyboard built in? Or a shirt that lights up?

In Dubai, its already possible to take the subway without anyone driving it!

A driverless subway in Dubai.

Driverless cars

There are already electric cars on the roads, but in the next few years, cars that don't need a driver may be a common sight! Several companies have already produced cars with a huge number of electronic sensors, and enough computing power to drive themselves safely on public roads. Who knows, one day soon you may be able to read this book in a car that's automatically taking you where you want to go!

Try It Yourself

Trick cling wrap!

Electrical charges can attract or repel each other. You can easily demonstrate this (and play a trick on someone at the same time!).

Unroll some cling wrap and then roll it back up. You will see that it sticks to itself. Next, unroll a bit of cling wrap, cut off a thin strip, and hang it over the middle finger of one hand. (You might need an adult to help you.) Take your other middle finger and rub it down the inside surfaces of the two dangling pieces of cling wrap. Presto! The ends of the cling wrap will now repel each other.

Now you can show it to your parents and tell them they've bought faulty cling wrap!

Make a magnet

You can make your own magnet. The only catch is you need a magnet to do it!

Find a magnet and a piece of iron. An iron nail would work well, but make sure you ask permission to use it before beginning this experiment. Run the magnet along the iron nail in the same direction twenty to thirty times. If it's a horseshoe magnet, only use one end of it.

Your iron nail is now magnetized, and you have a magnetic nail! It's as easy as that!

Make a fruit battery

You will need:

Wire (copper is best)

2 nails

2 lemons

Masking tape

A solar-powered calculator

2 pennies

What to do:

Ask an adult to help you with the following:

1. Take the battery out of the calculator and cover the solar cell with masking tape so no light reaches it.
2. Get an adult to help you cut three pieces of wire about 6 inches (15 cm) long each.
3. Wrap the end of a wire around one penny.
4. Cut a small slit in one lemon and push the wire-wrapped penny halfway in.
5. Wrap another piece of wire around the second penny in the same way, but wrap the other end of the wire around one of the nails. Cut a slit in the second lemon to push in the second penny. Push the nail into the first lemon.
6. Wrap one end of the final wire around the other nail and push it into the second lemon.
7. If you touch the two free ends of wire to the contact points in the battery compartment of the calculator, the calculator should come on! This can be a bit tricky, so don't give up! The lemon is acting as a battery, and you have built a circuit for the electricity to flow around.

You can find a demonstration of what to do at:

www.youtube.com/watch?v=AY9qcDCFeVI

Design an electronic quiz board

You will need:

A pair of scissors with points, or a hole punch

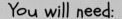

A piece of cardboard

Sticky tape

A flashlight bulb

Aluminum foil

A 9-volt battery

A list of quiz questions and answers. The questions can be on any subject, but why not try making up some questions and answers based on what you've discovered from this book?

3 wires

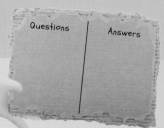

Questions | Answers

What to do:

1. Draw a line down the middle of the cardboard.

2. Write your questions on one side of the line.

3. Write the answers on the other side of the line. Mix up the positions of the answers so each is not directly opposite the question it is answering.

Questions	Answers
Question 1	Answer a
Question 2	Answer b
Question 3	Answer c
Question 4	Answer d
Question 5	Answer e
Question 6	Answer f

4. Get an adult to help you make a hole beside each question and each answer with the scissors or hole punch.

5. Cut some thin strips of aluminum foil about half an inch (one cm) wide.

6. Turn the card over, and stick a strip of foil down with tape so that it connects the hole beside the first question with the hole beside its correct answer. It's important that the foil is completely covered with tape.

7. Repeat for each question-and-answer pair.

8. Turn the card over. You should be able to see the foil through each hole.

9. Connect the wires, bulb, and battery as shown.

10. To use the quiz board, press the end of one wire to the foil beside question one, and the other wire to the foil beside an answer. If your answer is wrong, nothing happens. If you are right, the bulb will light up!

Timeline

 Electricity!

1600:
William Gilbert first uses the term "electricity."

1820:
Hans Christian Oersted finds that electricity and magnetism are related.

1878:
Thomas Edison invents an improved lightbulb.

1780:
Luigi Galvani discovers that electricity makes muscles twitch.

1820:
André-Marie Ampère publishes a combined theory of electricity and magnetism.

1865:
James Clerk Maxwell figures out the math behind electromagnetism.

400 BC:
Democritus proposes the theory that all matter is made of atoms.

 1800

0   1600

1747:
Benjamin Franklin discovers there are two types of charges and names them positive and negative.

1831:
Michael Faraday invents the electric motor.

600 BC:
Thales of Miletus describes what we now call static electricity.

1790:
Alessandro Volta invents the first battery.

1882:
Edison switches on the first DC generator supplying power to customers.

58

1897:
J.J. Thomson discovers the electron.

1943:
Tommy Flowers develops the first electric programmable computer, called Colossus.

1957:
Bardeen, Brattain, and Shockley win the Nobel Prize for Physics for inventing the transistor.

1967:
First handheld calculator is invented by a team led by Jack Kilby.

1973:
First cell phone is released by Motorola.

2014:
Isamu Akasaki, Hiroshi Amano, and Shuji Nakamura are awarded Nobel Prize for Physics for creating blue light LED.

Electrons

2000

1900

1972:
First home video games are introduced.

1947:
John Bardeen, Walter Brattain, and William Shockley invent the transistor.

1978:
Space Invaders game is launched.

1958:
Jack Kilby invents the integrated circuit.

Find Out More

Visit

The Franklin Institute in Philadelphia, PA, traces the path of electricity from a power plant to an outlet.
https://www.fi.edu/exhibit/electricity

The Spark Museum of Electrical Invention in Bellingham, WA, features a giant Tesla Coil that produces lightning bolts up to nine feet (2.7 m) long!
http://www.sparkmuseum.org

Try the static electricity generator at the Ontario Science Centre in Toronto, ON.
http://bit.ly/1EsQEyP

Read

Hydroelectric Power: Power from Moving Water (Energy Revolution). Marguerite Rodger. Crabtree Publishing Company, 2010.

What Are Electrical Circuits? (Understanding Electricity). Ronald Monroe. Crabtree Publishing, 2012.

What Are Insulators and Conductors? (Understanding Electricity). Jessica Pegis. Crabtree Publishing, 2012.

What Is Electricity? (Understanding Electricity). Ronald Monroe. Crabtree Publishing, 2012.

What Is Electromagnetism? (Understanding Electricity). Lionel Sandner. Crabtree Publishing, 2012.

Log on to

Fun facts show how electricity gets from a power plant to your home.
http://bit.ly/1ROiSLM

This site helps further explain magnetic fields.
http://bit.ly/1QTkAdT

This activity helps you "see" a magnet's magnetic field.
http://bit.ly/2fDC06P

Watch science demonstrations about electricity and magnetism, play games, and take quizzes.
http://bit.ly/2e9EFnD

Glossary

alloy Metal made of a mix of two or more different metals

amp (ampere) Unit used to measure electric current

atom The smallest part of an element; A building block from which everything is made up

capacitor A device that can store electrical energy

chemical element A substance that can't be broken down into a simpler form

circuit A closed path that an electric current can follow

concept An idea or a thought

core The innermost part

DNA The material that carries all the information needed for a living thing to develop

electric chair A method of killing a criminal by strapping them to a chair and electrocuting them

electricity Energy resulting from charged particles

electron A small particle that has a negative charge within an atom

element A pure substance that contains a single type of atom

emitting Giving off

exposure Being unprotected, left open

fluorescent Gives out visible light when exposed to invisible ultraviolet light

fossil fuels Fuels (such as oil, gas, or coal) formed from the remains of plants and animals that died millions of years ago

generator A device that changes mechanical energy into electrical energy

geophysicists A scientist who studies the earth using gravity, as well as magnetic, seismic, and electrical methods

greenhouse gases Gases (such as carbon dioxide) that trap the Sun's heat in the atmosphere, making Earth too warm

Higgs boson A recently observed particle

incandescent Giving out light when heated

inert Inactive; will not react with another chemical

lodestone Natural magnetic mineral or type of iron ore

magnetism ctric charges resulting in repulsive and attractive forces between objects

magnetoreception A sense in some animals that allows them to detect magnetic fields

mass The amount of matter in an object or particle

molten Made into a liquid by heating

neutron A small particle that has no charge within an atom

nuclear power Energy released by splitting atoms

nucleus The center of an atom

ore A mineral that contains metal

pacemaker A small electrical machine put inside someone to make their heart beat evenly

particle A tiny piece of matter

philosopher Someone who studies ideas about the meaning of life

pixels Tiny dots that make up the picture on a computer or television screen

preserved Kept in its original state

proton A small particle that has a positive charge within an atom

radiation Energy released from something; Many types of radiation are dangerous

radioactive Releasing a type of energy called radiation

repel Force objects to move apart

rotation Complete turn around a central point

solar From the Sun

static electricity Electricity that builds up in one place, rather than flowing as a current

toxic Poisonous

transformer A device that increases or decreases the voltage of electrical energy

transistor An electronic switch

tungsten A hard, gray metal used to make the wire in lightbulbs

turbine A machine that produces electricity when fast-flowing water, steam, gas, or air makes its wheel or rotor turn

vaporized Made into vapor, or small drops of liquid mixed with air

volt A unit of measurement in electricity

Index